GIFTED FOR Exploit

DARE JESSE OGUNDELE

GIFTED FOR EXPLOIT

DARE JESSE

GIFTED FOR EXPLOIT

ISBN: 978-978-783-042-0

Printed and published in Nigeria by
G&MPrint
#2 Oke Street, Opp. Diamond Estate Gate,
Diamond B/Stop, off Lasu/Igando Road,
Isheri-Olofin, Lagos, Nigeria.

mtunkajo@yahoo.com
0805 612 5919

CONTENTS

DEDICATION

I dedicate this book to the Almighty God for granting me the wisdom to create this divine masterpiece

ACKNOWLEDGEMENT

I'm grateful for the guidance and mentorship I've received over the years from my spiritual father, **Rev. Dr. Tunde Kajogbola,** which has been instrumental in this project. My heartfelt thanks go to Pastor Bisi Adewale for his invaluable impartation.

I also want to express my appreciation to Pastor Joshua Ogundele (biological father) for his guidance. The efforts of dedicated youth executive cannot be overemphasized especially Yemitan Hannah, whose unwavering support played a crucial role in bringing this book project to fruition.

First Word

A man's gift maketh room for him, and bringeth him before great men. (Proverbs 18:16)

George MacDonald tells of a castle in which lived an old man and his son. Although they owned the castle, they were so poor they could scarcely get bread to keep from starving, yet within the castle were concealed, by ancestors, for future necessity, very costly jewels. Although close to abundance, they were starving and living in abject poverty because they knew nothing about the concealment of wealth meant for them.

So it is in our world today. We are loaded with gifts, abilities and potentials unleashed, yet stranded. This is because we know not who we are, what lies inside us and why we are on earth.
This book (you are holding in your hands presently)** will help unravel the mysteries shrouded in our existence. You are more than who you think you are.

* It will help reveal the hidden potentials inside of you.
* It will also help bring your goals and dreams into reality.

This is my heart's desire for many. I have seen so many in the world

today, who blame people for their predicament. They say words like, "if I had come from a rich family, my life would have been better than this." Some say, life is unfair to them and that they are unlucky. Is this really true?
The wise one once said: "I returned and saw under the sun that - The race is not to the swift, Nor the battle to the strong, Nor bread to the wise, Nor riches to men of understanding, Nor favor to men of skill; But time and chance happen to them all. (Ecclesiastes 9:11)

Like the castle filled with wealth that is not discovered, that's the same with thousands out there. It is time to stop pointing accusing fingers and start looking inwards by giving answers to questions that would transform your life.

It is important to know that for every purpose in life, there is a timing dimension. Now is the time to awake from every form of sleep and slumber and begin to take the matter of your destiny with utmost importance.

Therefore He says: "Awake, you who sleep, Arise from the dead, And Christ will give you light." (Ephesians 5:14)

This is the time of discovery. You have to be intentional about it this time. YES! You have been looking at the same thing as everyone else but now you have to think differently.

The greatest obstacle of discovery is not ignorance, rather, it is the illusion of knowledge. This requires you unlearning what you think is right and relearning new things that would bring about change and transformation.

The beginning of true knowledge itself is the discovery of something you do not know or understand.

One of the ways to find answers is engaging in the process of self-discovery. Indeed! There is no greater journey than the one that you must take to discover the mysteries that lie within you.

Failure to discover, is failure along the whole path of life and that of greatness. I love the way the Bible in Basic English puts it. It says ***"Destruction has overtaken my people because they have no knowledge; because you have given up knowledge, I will give you up …" (Hosea 4:6)***

Acquiring knowledge is a choice. No one will force you to it. God revealed to us the cause of destruction. He says "Knowledge", if a man fails to acquire knowledge, what becomes of him? There is no way such a man can be helped.

It is the pathway to transformation. Every great man has gone through that path. Those aspiring to be great are also walking in this path. Are you aspiring to be great? You also should begin your journey today on this path.

Join me as we journey together in this pathway of the knowledge of self-discovery.

CHAPTER ONE

GOD'S MASTERPIECE

Psalm 33:15 - He fashions their hearts individually; He considers all their works.

Leonardo da Vinci artwork on "The Last Supper" is undoubtedly one of the most important of art of all times. This magnificent work of art has been seen by Leonardo's contemporary artists as the "Painting that Speaks", something that had never happened before. The Last Supper painting is a snapshot of the moment Christ tells his Apostles that one of them will betray him. The painting depicts each apostle reacting in his own unique way.

The Last Supper took da Vinci three years to complete. He didn't use the normal style because he wanted to achieve something grandeur. The artwork became a masterpiece because it was his greatest work. This singular work by Leonardo also had impact on artists of all ages.

The Last Supper became a masterpiece because of the effort placed on it and the innovative approach used by the artist.

Like Da Vinci's Last Supper, You are God's masterpiece, wonderfully and fearfully created.
I will praise thee, for I am fearfully and wonderfully made. (Psalm 139:14)

At creation, God put together every of his best resources to create you. You are not an accidental creation, rather you were created with masterly skill. It takes a master, to create a masterpiece. In fact, you are God's greatest piece of His creation.

The beauty about God's creation is in its uniqueness. No two humans are genetically identical. These undivided differences are the key to techniques such as your genetic finger printing, the texture of your skin, the way you think and even the way you walk. It is discovered that no two people have ever been found to have the same finger prints. Including identical twins. You are unique.

THE BLUE PRINT

A blueprint is something which acts as a plan, model, or template for others. It can also be referred to as;

- A Design
- A Master Plan
- A Program
- A Strategy
- An Arrangement
- A Ground Plan
- A Scheme
- A Project

God told one of his masterpieces... *"Before I formed you in the womb I knew you. Before you were born I sanctified you. I ordained you a prophet to the nations."*

This is the blueprint behind your creation. We could see a pre-existing relationship, an intent and also an appointment.

Let's Examine God's Blueprint for Creation

This will serve as a guide in helping us to understand and value God's creation.
During creation, God had a master plan and layout. Here's God's blue print for HIS MASTERPIECE CREATION

1. PRE-EXISTING RELATIONSHIP BEFORE TIME

Before I formed you in the womb I knew you..... (Jeremiah 1:5)

God had a knowledge of you before you came into existence. The knowledge of God for your life did not begin after your birth. It began even before you were formed in the embryo.

Every creature already had a pre-existing relationship with God before time. He was intentional about your creation. Your height, complexion and every of the features you possess is according to his blueprint. Isn't this great? Through divine will, your future have been determined. The life of Rebekah's sons were determined by God even before they were born. When the mother of these boys was pregnant, she felt a struggle within her and pondered why it was so. Genesis 25:22-23 records *"But the children struggled together within her; and she said, "If all is well, why am I like this?" So she went to inquire of the LORD. And the LORD said to her: "two nations are in your womb, Two peoples shall be separated from your body; One people shall be stronger than the other, And the older shall serve the younger."*

You must understand that before creation, your destiny have been perfected. He says,

"And we know that all things work together for good to them that love God, Now the presiding verse says; *to them who are called according to his purpose".*

It is worth noting that when you align with God's blueprint for your life, all things, not some things, will definitely work out for you. This is why you must discover and unravel God's blueprint for your life.

Remember: You are wonderfully and fearfully created.

Whom He (God) did foreknow... God foreknew you before predestinating you.

2. CREATED WITH AN INTENT IN MIND.

Every masterpiece was created for a purpose. Every manufactured product was designed to meet the need and demand of man at a specific time. The manufacturer sees or envisage a problem, and in the quest to solving it, he starts with the product design, then comes the product. Many inventions were created to solve a specific problem or meet a certain need. The invention of the telephone was a response to the need of long distance communication.

We can as well use this to capture God's mind during creation. There is a problem on earth, God before time, designed the best piece to fix the problem.

Long before Jesus Christ came into this world, there was so much prophecy about his coming. The prophets of old saw the mind of God concerning the world and His plan for the redemption of man. So many due to this prophecy anticipated his coming. In other words, you were created with an intent in mind.

3. ORDINATION

"Before I formed you in the womb I knew you; before you were born I sanctified you; I ordained you a prophet to the nation." (Jeremiah 1:5)

In God's master plan for your life, you have been appointed. He has set you apart for an office or duty. This appointment is by the virtue of a superior authority. It is a decree. The president of a country appoints ministers to function alongside him. This appointment comes with a responsibility. Every appointee knows the office to which he has been appointed. In fact, the presidents puts him in the area of his strength.

Then He appointed twelve, that they might be with Him and that He might send them out to preach. (Mark 3:14 NKJV)

Jesus appointed twelve to work with Him. Paul gives us an insight into this by saying:

For we are God's fellow-workers: ye are God's husbandry, God's building (1 Corinthians 3:9 ASV)

Dear friends, you are not accidentally created. You have been called and ordained by God as his fellow-worker.

Praise God! Hallelujah!!!

You are God's masterpiece according to his blueprint.

CHAPTER TWO

CREATION GROANS

For all creation, gazing eagerly as if with outstretched neck is waiting and longing to see the manifestation of the sons of God. (Romans 8:19)

Helen Kellen was born in 1880. At a young age, she became deaf and blind due to an illness. With the help of her dedicated teacher, Anne Sullivan, Keller learned to communicate through touch and developed a rich understanding of language. She excelled academically and graduated from college, becoming the first deaf-blind person to earn a Bachelor of Arts degree.

Keller promoted autonomy by showing that one's impairments need not limit their potential. She increased awareness and understanding of the challenges individuals with disabilities experienced by publicity and travelling widely.
Creation is earnestly waiting for what is embedded inside of you to be unleashed. Until it is unleashed, the groaning's would not stop or cease.

At the time of Helen Keller, the disabled were believed to be hopeless, having nothing to offer to the world but Keller changed the narrative. She was able to identify the groaning's of the creation.

She became a voice that was heard all over the world today despite her deafness. Helen Keller was unable to hear or see, yet she nevertheless made important strides in resolving crucial difficulties.

Another who responded to creation's groaning is "The shepherd boy" who later became the king of Israel. The people needed a savior. There was so much fear, confusion and pain in the land. Then came the manifestation of a son, David.

What is inside of you is not limited to you alone. God deposited them intentionally to answer the groaning's of humanity. You are a solution to the world's problem.

Here's a better way to understand this.

Matthew, one of the apostles of Jesus Christ, recounts a significant passage: ***"The land of Zebulun and the land of Naphtali, by the way of the sea, beyond the Jordan, Galilee of the gentiles. The people who sat in darkness have seen a great light, and upon those who sat in the region and shadow of death light has dawned" (Matthew 4:15-16)***

There was a time when a portion of the land of Israel and beyond was plunged into profound darkness. It was a period marked by chaos, affliction, poverty, pain, sorrow, death, and hunger. In this context, darkness symbolized all the hardships mentioned. The devil held sway over their lives.

In response to their cries and pain, God sent Jesus Christ, His Son, much like He has sent you to answer their pleas. Did Jesus respond to the cries of creation? Indeed, He did. Matthew's testimony asserts, ***"The people saw a great light."*** Jesus actively addressed the groans of creation.

My dear friend, what are you waiting for? It's time to reveal your true potential. It's time to step out of your comfort zone. It's time to become that brilliant beacon of hope to which you are destined to shine.

Understanding the Lamentations of Creation and failing to comprehend the cries of creation could hinder your ability to solve the world's problems to which you have been called.

Understanding Creation Groaning

If you don't understand how creation groans, you might not be able to solve the world's problem to which you have being sent to.

Groaning through Burdens

Now it happened in the process of time that the king of Egypt died. Then the children of Israel groaned because of the bondage, and they cried out; and their cry came up to God because of the bondage. (Exodus 2:23)

Your burdens are signs that creation is groaning. It is a sign that a person or a group are in pains. You must learn to listen because therein lies its voice. It speaks through it to you. These are creation's means of communication. These burdens come to you through an unusual and unexplainable feelings. You feel worried over matters concerning people yet you cannot explain why that feeling is coming.

How Do We Respond To Creation Groaning?
Now it came to pass in those days, when Moses was grown, that he went out to his brethren and looked at their burdens. And he saw an Egyptian beating a Hebrew, one of his brethren. So he looked this way and that way, and when he saw no one, he killed the Egyptian and hid him in the sand. (Exodus 2:11-12)

Moses had a burden inside of him but he didn't know the way out. The best option he had was by killing the Egyptian. Do you carry out God's purpose by killing? Obviously, the answer is no.

Here are guides to help discern and respond to groaning's.
1. Learn to listen
You must learn to listen. Learning the art of attentive listening is imperative. These burdens often manifest in the form of:

Internal Struggles: Consider Moses, who dwelt among his brethren despite being raised in the opulence of the king's palace. Witnessing their mistreatment during his walks among them stirred something profound within him. In the solitude of his private moments, he contemplated their suffering, and this led him to shed tears.
Moses lived in the midst of his brethren even though he was

nurtured and brought up in the king's palace. He saw how they were treated. Whenever he goes out and walk in the midst of them, he had this unusual feeling. He had compassion on them. I could perceive that in his closet the thought of how they feel comes to him which caused him to weep.

Discovering your purpose on earth most times always start with a feeling to solve people's problem. Moses had a feeling and a burden to save this people but he did not know how. Recognizing and responding to creations groaning begins by listening to difficult concern dwelling within you.

Nehemiah serves as another remarkable example. His feelings and emotions acted as a compass, guiding him toward a divine purpose. Your emotions often serve as a conduit through which the world communicates with you.

And it came to pass in the month of Nisan, in the twentieth year of King Artaxerxes, when wine was before him, that I took the wine and gave it to the king. Now I had never been sad in his presence before. (Nehemiah 2:1)
In essence, the path to understanding and addressing the world's needs commences with a willingness to listen to the profound concerns that reside within your heart.

The Cry of Humanity's Pain:
Nehemiah's response to creation's groans was deeply rooted in his attentiveness to the suffering of his people:

They said to me, "The survivors who are left from the captivity in the province are there in great distress and reproach. The wall of Jerusalem is also broken down, and its gates are burned with fire." (Nehemiah 1:3)

When you remain unmoved by the pain of others, it signifies that you may not have been sent to them. The Scriptures recount Jesus' example, stating, *"And when Jesus went out He saw a great multitude; and He was moved with compassion for them, and healed their sick." (Matthew 14:14)*

Compassion for people compels you to respond to their needs. Just as Jesus solved the problems of the people based on His compassion, you should also follow suit. Consistently look for signs of others' distress; it's an indicator that you have a calling to assist them. Compassion motivated Jesus to heal the sick and provide food for the multitude:
"Then Jesus went about all the cities and villages, teaching in their synagogues, preaching the gospel of the kingdom, and healing every sickness and every disease among the people. But when He saw the multitudes, He was moved with compassion for them because they were weary and scattered, like sheep having no shepherd." (Matthew 9:35-36)

In our generation, there's an urgent need for individuals to awaken from their slumber and actively respond to the cries of creation. Jesus also emphasized the scarcity of laborers, saying, *"The harvest truly is plentiful, but the laborers are few. Therefore pray the Lord of the harvest to send out laborers into His harvest." (Matthew 9: 37-38)*

The Call to Action

Now is the moment to rouse from your slumber. There's no place left for procrastination. You hold the solution to the cries of creation within you.

Isaiah 60:1 implores us to *"Arise, Shine... for our light has come."*

Consider for a moment what would have occurred if Jesus had not responded to the people. It's evident that they would have continued to suffer in their predicaments.

It's vital to recognize that each time a child is born into this world, they are sent with a purpose—to solve a problem. In the case of God's people in bondage, they could no longer endure their plight and cried out to God. Their cries reached the heavens, but we know that God doesn't descend from the heavens to directly address human problems. Instead, He employs individuals.

Every groan is a manifestation of a problem faced by humanity, as previously discussed in Chapter one. You are God's masterpiece, intricately designed to provide solutions to these problems.

Let this truth resonate deeply within you:

"I am the solution to humanity's problems. I am sent to respond to the cries of creation."

CHAPTER THREE

SUCH A TIME AS THIS?

For if you remain completely silent at this time, relief and deliverance will arise for the Jews from another place but you and your father's house will perish. Yet who knows whether you have come to the kingdom for such a times as this? (Esther 4:14)

Your existence in the world now is God's perfect timing for you. It begins with your biological parents, who gave birth to you, the place and the time. Many a times, I hear people cursing the day they were born even the parents who gave birth to them. They echo the sentiments of Job, who said, ***"May the day perish on which I was born, and the night in which it was said, A male child is conceived" (Job 3:2)***

Some attribute their failure in life to the fact that their uncles, aunt and even father were irresponsible and exclaim, 'I despise my father; he is not a responsible man.'

While this may hold some truth, the fact remains that your arrival in this world is perfectly synchronized with God's plan. The challenge or obstacle before you may not be the issue itself, but rather, how you perceive it. Do you see it as a stepping stone to greatness or as what would weigh you down? What effort have you made to turn the situation around? Could it be that you are blinded by the problem and your failure and you are not able to see what God is doing through that situation?

It's time to shed the mentality that someone else is responsible for the setbacks you encounter in life. The sooner you grasp this truth, the better for you.

You have come to this world for such a time as this? When you take a closer look at the circumstances, they may not appear favorable. There's chaos, the world is in crises, and the economy seems to deteriorate daily. The truth still remains, "You have come to this world for such a time as this?

Esther, a Jewish woman from the tribe of Benjamin was raised by her cousin Mordecai because she had no parents. Mordecai, who worked in the king's palace, played a significant role in Esther's life. He served as an adviser and supported her. Haman, who had hatred for the Jews (Esther's people) plan a plot to annihilate them.

However, Esther due to Mordecai's action was able to overcome their enemies. Esther's was brave and strategic in her action and this actions played a crucial role in averting the disaster that would have annihilated her people. Her actions were timely.

Invention, they say is the mother of necessity. We can testify or attest to the transformation that the invention of the light bulb has brought our world by a man named Thomas Edison. These needs brought about inventions and unrestricted thinking to inventors inventing.

CHAPTER FOUR

DREAM BIG; KEEP YOUR DREAMS ALIVE!

"And the Lord said unto Abram, after that Lot was separated from him, Lift up now thine eyes, and look from the place where thou art northward, and southward, and eastward, and westward. God told Abraham, for all the land which THOU SEETH, TO THEE WILL I GIVE IT, and to thy seed forever". (Genesis 13:14-15)

The inception of Disneyland traces back to a moment when Walt Disney expressed his vision for an amusement park while watching his daughters enjoy a carousel at Griffith Park in Los Angeles. As he observed his children at play and parents finding solace on a park bench, he dreamt of creating a place where families could bond and children could revel, all in a harmonious atmosphere.

During that era, conventional amusement parks weren't known for their family-friendly appeal. They often operated chaotically, had a reputation for overindulgence at the beer stands, and attracted an undesirable crowd. Disney aspired to revolutionize this norm.

For over 60 years, the "Happiest Place on Earth" has thrived as a small parcel of Southern California, known as Disneyland. Just one year after its inception, five million visitors flocked to the park. By 2019, over 700 million people had experienced Disneyland's magic, with an annual attendance of more than 18 million.

Walt Disney, driven by the power of a dream, transformed 160 acres of land into an enchanted realm. In his own words, he revealed that the dream behind Disneyland began on a solitary park bench, while his daughters, Sharon and Diane, were still very young. During one of their regular Saturday outings, Walt sat on the sidelines munching on peanuts as his children reveled. As they circled on the merry-go-round, a brilliant idea dawned on him: "I felt that there should be something built, some sort of amusement enterprise built, where parents and children could have fun together."

Now is the time to dream big. Just as God instructed Abram to look and what he saw would become his possession, ***"The land which thou SEETH, to you will I give,"*** this concept can also be viewed from a different angle. If one cannot envision it, there's nothing to attain. Our sight sets the boundaries, and we cannot become what we haven't seen. The limitations in life are intrinsically linked to the scope of our dreams.

As someone once stated, "Imagination sets the course for your destination," and the wise saying holds true, "***For as the thoughts of his heart are, so is he***" (Proverbs 23:7). Your imagination paves the path to success, and what you cannot envision will not materialize. Imagination wields immense power. You are presently where you are due to your imagination. The moment you start seeing, you start becoming.

"For as the thoughts of his heart are, so is he."

Walt Disney's journey began with a vision, and he famously stated, ***"If you can dream it, you can do it."*** Your failure to create or become stems from either not dreaming big enough or not dreaming at all.

The life of Walt Disney teaches us several lessons. First, it doesn't matter where you start; what matters is that you begin. Regardless of your current position in life, keep moving forward. The only obstacle that can truly hinder your progress is yourself.

THOUGHTS AND DREAMS: THE POWER WITHIN

Walt Disney, a visionary, left us with invaluable wisdom:

1. "If you can dream it, you can do it. Always remember that this whole thing was started by a mouse." - WALT DISNEY
2. "All our dreams can come true if we have the courage to pursue them." - WALT DISNEY
3. "Ask yourself if what you are doing today will get you where you want to go tomorrow." - WALT DISNEY

What occupies your daily thoughts? What do you envision for yourself?

In the Book of Numbers, God instructed Moses to send twelve men, one from each tribe of Israel, to spy out the land of Canaan—a land promised to them. Upon their return, they presented their findings. They acknowledged that the land indeed flowed with milk and honey and displayed its fruitful bounty. However, ten of the spies expressed fear, emphasizing the strength of the inhabitants, the fortified cities, and the presence of giants—the descendants of Anak.

But two of the spies, Joshua and Caleb, maintained a positive outlook. They urged the people to move forward and take possession of the land. They believed in what they had seen.

The ten fearful spies, on the other hand, let their imaginations run wild. They painted a grim picture, describing the land as one that consumed its inhabitants, where everyone was of great stature. They even compared themselves to grasshoppers in their own eyes, as well as in the eyes of the giants.

Regrettably, the negative imagination of the majority prevented them from entering the Promised Land. In fact, they all perished in the wilderness, except for Joshua and Caleb.

How do you perceive your life? Do you view yourself as a grasshopper? Many people lack belief in their own dreams and visions, often falling into the trap of comparison. However, comparing oneself to others is unwise, as it can hinder personal growth and vision fulfillment.

2 Corinthians 10:12 reminds us, *"For we dare not class ourselves or compare ourselves with those who commend themselves. But they, measuring themselves by themselves and comparing themselves among themselves are not wise."*

When God imparts a vision, your role is to believe in it and act upon it. Comparing your God-given vision to others can stifle its potential. Such comparisons can lead to self-doubt and fear, inhibiting you from realizing your true potential.

In conclusion, embrace your unique vision, trust in it, and remember the wisdom of Walt Disney: "If you can dream it, you can do it." Don't let the fear of giants or the allure of comparison hold you back from achieving your dreams.

FACTS ABOUT YOUR DREAMS

1. Your Dreams, Visions, and Ideas Are Seeds

Think of your dreams, visions, and ideas as seeds. Just like planting a seed in the ground, you must nurture them. Some seeds take time to germinate, possibly months or even years. Your dream might fall into the category of those that require years of care and patience. It's essential to invest time and effort into nurturing them.

2. Your Dreams, Visions, and Ideas Are Unique

Each person's dreams, visions, and ideas are unique and special. They are gifts from God, tailored specifically for you. Believe in the uniqueness of your dreams, and remember that they were entrusted to you for a reason.

3. Action Is Required to Realize Your Dreams

Merely conceiving or imagining your dreams is not enough. To turn them into reality, you must take action. Action is the bridge between your dreams and their fulfillment. Your determination and effort are the keys to bringing your dreams to life.

Poser: WHAT ARE YOUR DREAMS LIKE?

Take a moment to reflect on your dreams. What are they like? Are they seeds waiting to be planted and nurtured? Do you believe in their uniqueness and divine origin? Are you taking the necessary actions to transform them into reality? Your dreams are your potential waiting to be unleashed, so seize the opportunity to make them come true.

CHAPTER FIVE

YOU'VE GOT ALL IT TAKES!

"Look, I have seen a son of Jesse the Bethlehemite, who is skillful in playing, a mighty man of valor, a man of war, prudent in speech, and a handsome person, and the LORD is with him". (1 Samuel 16:18)

You have all you need to be who you are. No man here on earth is born empty. Everyone is born with potentials awaiting to be unleashed. You are equipped with everything you need to fulfil God's purpose for your life. Take a look at yourself and you are naturally like what you are supposed to be and do. What you love to do naturally is usually what you were born to do.

- You've got all it takes! You are too loaded to be stranded.
- You've got all it takes to be great in life. You are unstoppable. The only person that can stop you is YOU.

Reasons Why People Fail In Life:

1. **Failure to Realize Their Importance:** Some individuals fail because they don't recognize their significance and the

importance of their actions.

2. **Underestimating Their Usefulness:** Underestimating your own usefulness while overestimating that of others can hinder your success.
3. **Comparison:** Comparing oneself to others can be a destructive force that hampers one's destiny.
4. **Focusing on Weaknesses:** Concentrating on weaknesses rather than strengths can limit personal growth and achievement.
5. **The Fear of Starting:** Fear can paralyze potential, preventing individuals from taking the first step towards their goals.

KEYS TO UNLOCKING YOUR ABILITY

DISCOVERY

Socrates says an unexamined life is not worth living. To discover means to find or learn something for the first time. It also means to expose, uncover. There is so much encapsulated or embedded within you that needs to be uncovered. The reason why so many people are lost in life is simply because they don't know what lies inside of them. Discovery is the key to performance.

A prime example of the power of self-discovery is King David. He didn't ascend to kingship solely because of his anointing; rather, he understood his identity and purpose. This self-awareness empowered him to confront Goliath fearlessly.

Scripture describes David as ***"skillful in playing, a mighty man of valor, a man of war, prudent in speech, and a handsome person."***

Each of David's skills and attributes was directed toward fulfilling his purpose and destiny.

The crucial question to ask yourself is, "What am I skilled at?" ** Identifying your strengths and talents is essential for navigating life's course effectively. It's challenging to chart a meaningful life path if you are unsure of your destination. To lead a purposeful life, allocate time for self-discovery. What you know about yourself is what you can act upon. Take stock of your unique gifts and abilities; they hold the key to unlocking your full potential. Self-discovery is the foundation upon which you can build a life filled with meaning and significance.

BUILD AND DEVELOP YOUR ABILITIES

After discovery, the next step is development. It is not enough to identify your gifts, skills, and abilities; you must be intentional about honing and improving them.

Consider the example of David during his time in the wilderness. He didn't squander those moments of solitude; instead, he actively worked on developing his leadership skills and enhancing his musical talents. As someone aptly put it:

"Preparation + Opportunities = Favor."

So many pray for favor, wish for opportunities but when both present themselves, they aren't prepared for it. Rather, they mess it up.

When the door of opportunity and favor opened up for David, he was prepared for it. He knew what to do at all times. This is what preparation does. You will always know what to do per time. You have an understanding of the job which the end point leads to excellence.

This phase of development demands intentionality. Nothing occurs by chance; you must actively pursue growth and improvement.

HOW DO YOU DEVELOP THESE ABILITIES?

1. **Reading: Continuously educate yourself.** Reading opens doors to knowledge and helps you stay informed about your field or area of interest.

2. **Training:** Seek out training opportunities to enhance your skills and abilities. This might involve formal education, workshops, seminars, or hands-on experience.

Remember, development is an ongoing process that requires dedication and effort. By investing in yourself through reading and training, you empower yourself to excel in your chosen path and make the most of the opportunities that come your way.

BELIEVE IN YOURSELF

Belief is a very powerful tool in unlocking one's ability. If you fail to believe yourself, no one is committed to believe in you. It is what you believe that you act on.

Those who try to become like someone else are those who either haven't discovered themselves or do not believe in who they are or what they have. This is an unsafe way to live especially in making impact on earth.
One of the keys to overcoming fear is to know that you are equipped with everything you need to fulfil your purpose.

Here's Paul's word to Young Timothy:

For God hath not given us the spirit of fear; but of power, and of love, and of a sound mind.

Fears to overcome

1. Fear of the unknown
2. Fear of failure or failing
3. Fear of what people would say

IGNORE YOUR WEAKNESS AND BASK IN YOUR STRENGTH

The only person who is omniscient and omnipotent is God. He is the only one without limitation or any weakness. God created mankind with diversities. He did not put all the potentials into one person. He designed each person for their purpose and that design is perfect.

Your design is God's best for you. He designs you the way he wants* you to function and that is your strength. So many times, we focus on the way we are not designed to function.

Those who are not designed to sing begin to envy those with the ability to sing. It is natural for you to covet the gifts of other people with great abilities but at the same time, you must acknowledge that certain areas are not your strength.

Make others as well covet your own gifting and abilities. In order to make this possible, you have to ignore your weaknesses.

STEPS TOWARDS DISCOVERY

1. **Ask God:** To uncover your purpose, seek guidance from the Creator, for He is the one who intricately designed you. Deuteronomy 29:29 reminds us that "the secret things belong to the Lord, but the things revealed belong to us and our children forever." God has the power to reveal deep and hidden insights, as stated in Daniel 2:22. Start your journey towards discovery by seeking His divine guidance.

2. **Do a Heart-Check:** Your heart holds clues to your purpose. Psalm 33:15 tells us that God fashions hearts individually, considering all their works. Perform a heart-check by asking yourself crucial questions:

    - **Predominating Desire:** What is your deepest desire? Often, your true purpose is linked to what you long for deeply. Your desires can guide you towards your calling.
    - **Passion:** Pay attention to what ignites your passion.

That "fire in the belly" can indicate an area where you have a divine assignment to make a difference.

- **Effectiveness:** Discover your areas of effectiveness. What are you naturally good at?

    - David was known for his skill in playing instruments,
    - Queen Esther's beauty and advocacy, saved the lives of her people.
    - Moses' leadership despite his stammering, and
    - Nehemiah's heart for rebuilding the wall, brought the exiles back to their city and made them recommit to God's law are all examples of individuals excelling in their areas of effectiveness.

3. **Take Stock of Your Skills:** As part of your journey towards discovery, recognize and nurture your skills. David's musical prowess, Esther's beauty, Moses' leadership despite his speech impediment, and Nehemiah's talent for rebuilding walls all played pivotal roles in their life purposes. What are you good at? Identify your unique talents and skills.

Remember that discovering your purpose is a process that requires introspection, seeking divine guidance, and recognizing the talents and desires that are deeply ingrained in your heart. Your journey toward purpose begins with a willingness to explore your innermost self and seek guidance from the Creator.

CHAPTER SIX

YOUR GIFT: USE IT OR LOSE IT

Therefore take the talent from him, and give it to him who has ten talents. For everyone who has, more will be given, and he will have abundance but from him who does not have, even what has he will be taken away. (Matthew 25:28-29)

Your talent is God's gift to you. What you do with it is your gift back to God says Leo Buscagalia. The parable of the talents is a powerful story to learn from (Matthew 25:14-30). Though, many might say it is just a story but I want you to know that it is more than a story. We can liken it to what is happening in the world today.

God, like the man who gave talents to his servants, has given gifts to every man on earth. These gifts are the instrument provided to fulfil your purpose. The discovery of these gifts is the key to fulfilment and performance.

These talents or gifts can be your musical ability, teaching skills, wisdom, charisma, giving, communication skills, dancing skills, writing ability, drawing and painting, or anything you are good at.

Without these gifts, there would be nothing to work with. In fact, life would be meaningless. It is like a builder or construction worker who claims to be an engineer yet he has no working tool. It's obvious that going to the site is a waste of time. This is the same with you. Your gift, talent, skills, abilities are all tools given to you by God to fulfil purpose.

God-given gifts are meant to be employed. Erma Bombeck's words carry profound wisdom: "when I stand before God at the end of my life, I would hope that I would not have a single bit of talent left, and could say, "I used everything God gave me." These words should serve as an ultimate aspiration for all of us as we journey through life. The saddest thing in life is a wasted talent.

A life filled with potentials and abilities yet not harnessed. If you fail to use it, you will lose it therefore don't let this God-given gifts to you gather dust.

Myles Munroe puts it this way:"DIE EMPTY". Apostle Paul went further to say of himself. ***"I have fought the good fight, I have finished the race, I have kept the faith."*** He said, 'I have finished the race'. So many at age sixty have not even started their race.

Life is a race. It takes those who are determined, focused and disciplined not to only finish the race but also win the prize set before them. This gives us an exposition on how our gifts are meant to be used. These gifts are to be used to benefit others.

Biblical Examples to learn from:

- The Psalmist used his musical skill to drive out the evil spirit in Saul. He also used his fighting skills to deliver God's people.

- Esther used her beauty and advocacy to deliver the Jews from annihilation.

- Nehemiah used his access to the king to rebuild the broken walls of Jerusalem.

- Paul used his eloquence to preach the gospel to the gentile.

•

What have you used your own skills or abilities for?

LOSS THROUGH CARELESSNESS

In the story of Samson, a Nazirite chosen by God to deliver the Israelites from the Philistines, we witness a remarkable example of someone blessed with extraordinary strength. Judges 14:5 recounts the astonishing feat where Samson tore apart a roaring lion with his bare hands. His strength was unique and unmatched, a divine gift from God.

However, as powerful as Samson was, he suffered a great downfall due to his own carelessness and sinful choices. Despite being destined to defeat the Philistines, he became a prey among them, languishing as a prisoner and grinding at a mill.

Samson's story is a poignant reminder of the consequences of carelessness. Despite his extraordinary gifts and divine calling, he lost it all due to his poor choices. It's a tragic narrative, but it holds valuable lessons for us all.

This indeed is pathetic!

WHAT ARE GIFTS?

GIFTS

Gifts are precious endowments, talents, or abilities bestowed upon us voluntarily and without charge. They can be natural talents or God-given abilities that set us apart. These gifts are intended for specific purposes, and understanding why they are given is crucial.

PURPOSE OF GIFTS

Gifts are given for a reason:

Purpose Fulfillment: They enable us to fulfill our God-given purpose and calling.
Service: Gifts empower us to serve others and make a positive impact on the world.

ENEMIES OF EXPLOITS

To achieve great exploits, we must overcome certain obstacles:

1. **Laziness**

Laziness is the habit of resting before exhaustion sets in. It's the act of procrastination, delaying today's work for tomorrow. Laziness is a formidable enemy of exploits, as it hinders progress and success. Proverbs 24:33 warns about the consequences of laziness and its link to poverty.

A little sleep, a little slumber, A little folding of the hands to rest; so shall your poverty come like a prowler, and your need like an armed man. (Proverbs 24:33)

2. **Fear (False Evidence Appearing Real)**

Fear is a paralyzing force that inhibits greatness. Believing in oneself is essential for achieving exploits. 1 John 4:18 highlights that fear torments and cripples, while perfect love casts out fear.

Fear inflicts pain on its host. You cannot be and live in fear and exercise your gifts effectively because you are being tormented. A life of fear is a life of anguish and misery. It is self-enslavement.

3. **Unbelief**

A lack of faith in one's abilities and the potential for success can be a significant hindrance to exploits.

4. **Complaining**

Complaining is a draining habit that saps energy and focus. Redirecting this energy towards positive pursuits is essential for growth and achievement.

5. **Indiscipline:**

A lack of discipline in areas of life have cost many. A life that wants to do exploits should be able to have control over his or her life. This includes your willingness to say no to acts and behavior when you ought to. This discipline should include the use of your time, the places you go, the things you do. Remember, what you do can simply make or mar you.

- **Lack of vision**

- **Distraction**

CHAPTER SEVEN

INSIGHT FOR EXPLOIT

And Elisha prayed, and said, "LORD, I pray, open his eyes that he may see." Then the LORD opened the eyes of the young man, and he saw. And behold, the mountains was full of horses and chariots of fire all around Elisha. (2 kings 6:17 NKJV)

It has been proven countless of times that whenever God wants to bless a man, He does not give material things such as money, rather, he gives ideas and insights. Insight is the ability or capacity to "see into". Mahinhim Forbes says, "The best Vision is Insight". Vision is a divine insight into God's plan for you.

Insight is the power to see what is not evident to the average mind. Insight is the capacity to gain an accurate and deep understanding of things. Sight is needed for heights. It is what differentiates the ordinary from the extraordinary. You need a picture for your future. What you cannot picture, you cannot capture.

Insight is the ability to have a clear, deep and sometimes sudden understanding of a complicated problem or situation.

Life is like a puzzle. It requires insight to be solved. When you envision the future you want for yourself, you are much more likely to take that step forward towards greatness.

If you don't have the slightest clue about your hopes, dreams and aspiration, then the chance toward exploit and greatness is NIL. Through insight, you are able to imagine that extraordinary feat is possible and that the ordinary could be transformed into something magnificent.

To have an insight is to imagine possibilities. This is the difference between those who do exploit and those who do not.

The greatest achievement of the human brain is its ability to imagine objects that do not exist in the real world. This ability allows us to think about the future. It is discovered that only 3% of the typical business person's time is spent thinking about the future. If you want your future to improve, you need insight.

Passion ignites insight. You don't see possibilities when you don't feel any passion. When you find something you truly believe in, that's the key.

And Elisha prayed, and said, "LORD, I pray, open his eyes that he may see." Then the Lord opened the eyes of the young man, and he saw. And behold, the mountain was full of horse and chariots of fire all around Elisha. (2 kings 6:17)

A life without insight is one lived with and in fear. A man without insight is one surrounded with abundance, riches and wealth yet cannot see. Like the young lad, until your eyes is opened, you cannot see. Every human being is potentially wealthy. To unleash and access wealth, insight is required.

THE IMPORTANCE OF INSIGHT

1. It puts an end to a life of a struggle. When you don't discover God's plan, you keep struggling.

2. Insight gives stability to your life. You know where you are heading. When you have vision, it prevents you from going anywhere you like, or following after what others are doing.

3. Insight gives you a definite focus

4. Insight gives direction to your life.

The future belongs to those who see the possibilities before they become obvious.

THE DIMENSIONS OF SIGHT

It is important we examine the dimensions of sight. This will help you gain more depth on this topic.

1. *EYESIGHT*

When the woman saw that the fruit of the tree was good for food

and pleasing to the eye, and also desirable for gaining wisdom, she took some and ate it. She also gave some to her husband, who was with her, and he ate it. Then the eyes of both of them were opened, and they realized they were naked; so they sewed fig leaves together and made coverings for themselves. (Genesis 3:6-7 NIV)

Eyesight, the most basic dimension of sight, is rooted in our physical senses. It relies on what we can perceive with our physical eyes, making it the lowest form of sight. However, this level of sight has limitations and can be deceptive. Decisions based solely on what is seen with the physical eyes may lead to misleading and destructive outcomes, as evidenced by the fall of Adam and Eve in the Garden of Eden.

2. FORESIGHT

Foresight is the ability to look ahead and consider the future. It involves thinking about and preparing for what lies ahead. Foresight is a critical ingredient for success, as it allows us to anticipate and shape the future.
FORESIGHT IS;

- Thinking the future
- Debating the future
- Shaping the future

Foresight is exemplified by Caleb's confidence in Numbers

13:30, where he believed in the possibility of overcoming challenges.

And Caleb stilled the people before Moses, and said, Let us go up at once, and possess it; for we are well able to overcome it. (Numbers 13:30)

Possibility is always attendant to foresight.

3. *HIND SIGHT*

For with thee is the foundation of life; in thy light shall we see light. (Psalm 36:9)

Hindsight involves reflecting on past events and understanding their significance and implications for the future. It's the application of lessons learned from history to navigate future situations. In Psalm 36:9, it is described as using the "light" of past experiences to illuminate the path forward. God's Word provides wisdom drawn from the past to guide us in the present and future.

4. INSIGHT

Insight is the ability to perceive the inner nature of things and see intuitively. It's often associated with seeing situations as God sees them. This dimension grants a deeper understanding of God's will and purpose. For instance, in 1 Kings 14:4-5, Ahijah receives insight from the Lord, allowing him to understand the true nature of Jeroboam's situation. Insight is considered the inner eye, the eye of authority, and it aligns with God's perspective.

Insight helps us to know the exact mind and will of God. We see what God is seeing. That's the power of this dimension. It is the inner eye; the eye of authority.

It is God's word that offers the wisdom and insight you need at every turn.

As you meditate, the lord gives us increased insight. The moment you begin to act on it, you enjoy prosperity and success. The word is full of insight and exploit.

Each dimension of sight offers a unique perspective, with eyesight serving as the foundation. Foresight empowers us to shape the future, hindsight applies lessons from the past, and insight provides a deeper understanding of God's will. It is through God's Word and meditation that we gain insight and wisdom to navigate life's challenges and pursue success.

HOW TO GAIN INSIGHT

Lack of ideas can be more limiting than a lack of money. Here are various ways to gain insight and generate valuable ideas:

1. **Change of Mind/Renewal of Mind** - As a Man Thinketh:
   - Eliminate negative thinking patterns.

   - Cultivate dissatisfaction with your current situation and embrace the belief that anything is possible.

- Recognize that there are untapped insights, thoughts, and ideas waiting to be discovered.

2. **Holy Spirit-Inspired Ideas**
   - Acknowledge God as the ultimate source of high-quality insights.
   - Stay connected to God to access superior ideas.
   - Being filled with God's spirit can lead to divinely inspired ideas that surpass human understanding.

3. **Definite Goals Inspire Insight:**
   - Having a clear and definite purpose in life fosters insight
   - Determine what you truly desire in life, and insights will come in alignment with your goals.
   - The level of insight often corresponds to the goals you set, and these insights can attract the necessary resources

4. **Identify a Need**
   - Look for unmet needs in your community or industry, and create solutions to fill those gaps.

5. **Adapt Another Idea**
   - Don't hesitate to modify and build upon existing ideas

to make them even better or more suitable for your context.

6. **Create a Need**
   - Innovate by introducing new products, services, or concepts that create a demand and address previously unconsidered needs.

7. **Exposure**
   - Broaden your horizons through reading, traveling, and exploring diverse experiences. Exposure to new environments and ideas can stimulate creativity.

8. **Prayer**
   - Seek divine guidance through prayer, as it can lead to inspiration and fresh ideas.

9. **Meditation on the Word of God**
   - The Bible, a rich source of wisdom and inspiration, showcases God's creativity. Meditating on its teachings can lead to profound insights.

Remember that the journey toward fulfillment may come with challenges, but persistence and patience are key. Success often comes when you transform your ideas into tangible realities.

CHAPTER EIGHT

TIME BOUND YOUR VISION

And the king said unto me, (the queen also sitting by him) for how long shall thy journey be? And when wilt thou return? So it pleased the king to send me; and I set him a time. (Nehemiah 2:6)

Every vision and responsibility should come with a defined timeframe. It's not sufficient to conceive a vision or shoulder a burden; you must establish a timeline to ensure its realization. I've witnessed numerous individuals with brilliant plans and divine inspiration that remained unrealized.

Take Nehemiah, for example. His vision was to rebuild the walls of Jerusalem, but before embarking on his journey toward fulfilling his destiny, he set a clear deadline. He made his vision time-bound.

Time-bounding your vision, goals, dreams helps:

- To ignite motivation
- To create a sense of urgency to achieve your vision.

Nehemiah's project was a SMART one, adhering to the SMART criteria:

- S - Specific
- M - Measurable
- A - Achievable
- R - Realistic
- T – Timely

1. SPECIFIC

Every divine vision and mission comes with a clear and distinct purpose. Just as God instructed Habakkuk in Habakkuk 2:2 to ***"write the vision, and make it plain upon tables, that he may run that readeth it,"*** we can see that every vision from God is well-defined and unambiguous. Consider God's directive to Abraham in Genesis 12:1-2, where He stated clearly, ***"Get thee out of thy country, and from thy kindred, and from thy father's house, unto a land that I will shew thee."*** The message was precise: ***"Go, and I will make thee a Great Nation."***

This clarity is also evident in the case of David. God instructed Samuel in 1 Samuel 16:16 to ***"Fill thine horn with oil, and go, I will send thee to Jesse the Bethlehemite. For I have provided me a king among his sons."*** Though the initial steps might be uncertain, obedience leads to revelation, and technical know-how often emerges once you take that first step. The Apostle Paul, too, received a specific purpose when the Lord told him in Acts 9:15 to "Go thy way: for he is a chosen vessel unto me, to bear my name before the Gentiles and kings, and children of Israel." Saul's vision and mission were distinct: to preach the gospel to the unsaved.

2. MEASURABLE

Progress can only be assessed when there are set measures in place. As Jesus mentioned in Luke 14:28, ***"For which of you, intending to build a tower, does not sit down first and count the cost, whether he has enough to finish it?"*** It is your responsibility to plan and understand what it takes to commence and complete your vision. While you trust God for guidance and resources, you play a vital role in realizing it. Nehemiah's actions, as seen in Nehemiah 2:7-9, illustrate this principle as he made meticulous plans, securing letters and resources for the rebuilding project.

Furthermore I said to the king, "If it pleases the king, let letters be given to me for the governors of the region beyond the River, that they must permit me to pass through till I come to Judah, and a letter to Asaph the keeper of the king's forest, that he must give me timber to make beams for the gates of the citadel which pertains to the temple, for the city wall, and for the house that I will occupy." And the king granted them to me according to the good hand of my God upon me. Then I went to the governors in the region beyond the River, and gave them the king's letters. Now the king had sent captains of the army and horsemen with me. (Nehemiah 2:7-9)

3. ACHIEVABLE

Divinely inspired visions, though grand, are attainable through faith. Throughout history, individuals who achieved remarkable feats were often ordinary people, but they had faith in the One who sent them. As Habakkuk 2:2 suggests, ***"For the vision is yet for an appointed time; But at the end of it will speak, and it will not lie. Though it tarries, wait for it, because it will surely come. It will not tarry."*** You must persevere and trust that any vision from God is achievable. Remember the saying, "God's will; God's bill," and learn to trust in the Lord.

You must be careful to follow through your God-given vision. Stand by it. Don't say because you are experiencing delay, you become discouraged and let go of the vision.

Take my yoke upon you and learn from me, for I am gentle and lowly in heart, and you will find rest for your souls. For my yoke is easy and my burden is light. (Matthew 11:29-30)

4. REALISTIC

God-given visions are authentic and genuine, as highlighted in Habakkuk 2:2, where God instructs, ***"Put the vision in writing and make it clear on stones so that the reader may go quickly."*** When you visualize it, believe it, and take action accordingly, you bring your vision closer to reality. Proverbs 6:21-22 emphasizes the importance of keeping your vision continually in your heart and mind, allowing it to guide your actions and decisions.

Bind them continually upon your heart; Tie them around your neck. (Proverbs 6:21)

What happens when you do this?

When you roam, they will lead you; when you sleep, they will keep you; and when you awake, they will speak with you. (Proverbs 6:22)

5. TIMELY

In 1960, late President Jack Kennedy of the United States, called scientists together and gave them ten years to make man to land on the moon. He was ready to give them every single dollar they needed. They accomplished the feat in nine years. Imposing a time constraint creates a sense of urgency and motivation. Without a specific timeframe, there may be a lack of momentum in pursuing your God-given vision. Therefore, time bounding your vision can lead to increased motivation and ultimately, achievement.

CHAPTER NINE

STAY THE COURSE

So my very dear friends, don't get thrown off course. Every desirable and beneficial gift comes out of heaven. The gifts are rivers of light cascading down from the Father of Light. There is nothing deceitful in God, nothing two-faced, nothing fickle. He brought us to life using the true word, showing us off as the crown of all his creatures. (James 1:16-18)

It's essential to acknowledge that every gift we manifest or possess is a divine bestowment from God, who is often referred to as "the Father of Light." One of the qualities we find in God is "Truthfulness." The above scripture says "There is nothing deceitful in God, nothing two-faced, nothing fickle."

If this is true of God that He gives gifts and He holds integrity with high esteem, our lives should align with this divine standard. It is expected of you to play your path by staying the course.

Staying the course involves persisting in our journey toward fulfilling our destiny, even when faced with adversity. We must not drift off course.

EVALUATING THE PROCESS: The Pathway to Greatness and Exploits.

1. IT ALL BEGINS WITH JESUS

Jesus said "I AM THE WAY".... (John 6:14)
Your journey towards greatness commences when you entrust the navigation of your life's vehicle to Christ. He is the Creator of humanity and the entire universe. Just as a product's manufacturer designs it to function in a specific way, God, through Jesus Christ, has appointed Him to guide and steer your life. His thoughts and plans towards you are thoughts of peace and not of evil, to give you a future and a hope. Your future and destiny are secured in Him.

Consider this instructive story about a man:
Many years ago, during the early part of the last century, a man's car broke down on the roadside. Despite his efforts, he couldn't get it to start. Then another man stopped to help. After a brief examination of the engine, the second man instructed the first to start the car, and it immediately roared to life. The car's owner asked in amazement, "How did you fix the car so quickly, and how did you know what it needed?" The man replied, "I am Henry Ford. I built the car. I know what makes it work."

Now is the time to entrust your destiny to the One who created you, who owns you, and who knows how to make your life work. Put an end to the futile efforts and gimmicks that have only seemed to worsen your situation day by day.

Consider this Scripture and glean wisdom from it: *Will the river-plant come up in its pride without wet earth? Will the grass get tall without water? When it is still green, without being cut down, it becomes dry and dead before any other plant. So it the end of all who do not keep God in mind; and the hope of the evil-doer comes to nothing. (Job 8:11-13)*

Everything on Earth has a source, just as the plant's source is the earth. Remove it from its source, and it withers.

Remember, **JESUS IS THE WAY.** Now that you know this, what will you do?

- ACCEPTANCE THROUGH CONFESSION

But what does it say? "The word is near you, in your mouth and in your heart" (that is, the word of faith which we preach): that if you confess with your mouth the Lord Jesus and believe in your heart that God has raised Him from the dead, you will be saved. (Romans 10:8-9)

As straightforward as this may sound, I emphasize the word simple. I encourage you to set this book aside for a moment and utter these words of prayer:
"Lord Jesus, I come to you in this hour. Have mercy on me. Forgive me for all my sins and cleanse me from all unrighteousness. Today, I accept you as my LORD and SAVIOR. Wash me thoroughly with your blood. In Jesus' name, I pray. AMEN."

Now that you have chosen to be with Jesus, it is imperative to stay the course by walking in the light of Christ.

2. LAY ASIDE EVERY WORK OF DARKNESS

What the Father expects of you is "truthfulness." There should be no trace of deceit within you. Remember that "Nothing deceitful is found in God," who is the giver of gifts. This means that whenever you manifest God's gifts in the world, it must be done with absolute truthfulness.

Consider Philippians 2:3, which advises, ***"Let nothing be done through selfish ambition or conceit, but in lowliness of mind let each esteem others better than himself."*** Some individuals possess gifts such as creative minds, strong communication abilities, writing skills, artistic talents, and more, but unfortunately, they use these gifts deceitfully. They use their creative talents to deceive, steal, and manipulate others.

The Holy Bible recounts the story of a man named Ahithophel, one of King David's most trusted advisers. It was said that ***"the advice of Ahithophel, which he gave in those days, was as if one had inquired at the oracle of God. So was all the advice of Ahithophel both with David and with Absalom." (2 Samuel 16:23)*** David's success and greatness can be traced back to Ahithophel because whenever David sought counsel or advice from him, he received words of wisdom that resolved his problems. Ahithophel's advice was divinely inspired.

However, Ahithophel, due to negative influences, became

deceitful. He played a key role in Absalom's rebellion against David, and his defection had a detrimental impact on David's kingdom. Whenever you engage in deceitful actions, destinies are adversely affected.

3. HOLD ON TO THE SOURCE

Our gifts and abilities come to life through the Word of God. The Word of God serves as the compass to navigate life's journey. Every traveler requires guidance. When a pilot flies a plane, how does he know the direction to his destination? One method is by using a magnetic compass. To reach their destination, pilots rely on maps and compasses. Without these tools, their journey becomes challenging, unclear, and uncertain.

Similarly, life's journey becomes difficult, unclear, and uncertain without our compass, which is "THE WORD OF GOD." Your destiny is like a treasure waiting to be discovered, and it is concealed within God's WORD. The Word of God serves the following purposes in our lives:

- It gives meaning to our lives.
- It provides us with direction.

As stated in Psalm 119:105, ***"Your word is a lamp to my feet and a light to my path."***

About the Author

Dare Jesse serves as the Youth Pastor at Grace Way Chapel International, where he has by the grace bestowed upon him demonstrated his pastoral leadership for three impactful years. His journey is adorned with remarkable achievements. He holds a diploma in Marine Engineering. Dare Jesse is currently pursuing a degree in computer science in Lagos State University with a degree in view from Savanna University of Missions(SUM)

Dare Jesse's life is a testament to his divine calling as an anointed minister of God, and his name is synonymous with remarkable accomplishments. He has demonstrated dynamic leadership abilities, channeled through fervent passion for the salvation of souls and the service of the Lord.

In God's unmerited favor, Dare Jesse resides in the vibrant city of Lagos, sharing this blessed journey with his loving family.

www.ingramcontent.com/pod-product-compliance
Lightning Source LLC
LaVergne TN
LVHW080628160826
845677LV00007B/1481

* 9 7 8 9 7 8 7 8 3 0 4 2 0 *